MINECRAFT™

NEW YORK

Copyright © 2021 by Mojang AB
Copyright © 2017 by Mojang AB and Mojang Synergies AB

Published in the United States by Del Rey, an imprint of Random House, a division of Penguin Random House LLC, New York.

DEL REY is a registered trademark and the CIRCLE colophon is a trademark of Penguin Random House LLC.

Originally published in the United Kingdom by Farshore, an imprint of HarperCollins Publishers, London.

ISBN 978-0-593-35583-1
Ebook ISBN 978-0-593-35584-8

Printed in China on acid-free paper

Written by Thomas McBrien

Illustrations by Ryan Marsh

randomhousebooks.com

2 4 6 8 9 7 5 3

Design by John Stuckey
Production by Laura Grundy

Special thanks to Sherin Kwan, Alex Wiltshire, Kelsey Howard and Milo Bengtsson.

MINECRAFT™

GUIDE TO CREATIVE

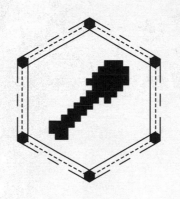

CONTENTS

HELLO

Welcome to *Minecraft: Guide to Creative!*

Minecraft is many things. It's a place to go on exciting adventures; it's a place to invent amazing things; it's a place to hang out with your friends. And it's also a place to build. We even made a mode that's just for letting your imagination go wild!

But everyone needs a little help with getting creative now and then, whether to learn new techniques or find inspiration. So we've put together this handbook of advice, suggestions, top tips and creative tricks.

These pages are filled with expert knowledge, so whether you're a beginner looking to get started or an experienced player seeking new challenges, there's something in here to help you become the builder you want to be.

This handbook is split into three sections. The first section will introduce you to Creative mode and guide you through the key elements of building creatively. Next, we'll look at various building techniques and how to combine blocks to create unique features. Lastly, we will look at how to apply your new skills with step-by-step build instructions.

LET'S GET CREATIVE!

CREATIVE 101

Minecraft is a sandbox game where anything is possible. Taking
your first step into the Overworld can be daunting, so take
a moment to familiarize yourself with the game. You will find
everything you need to know to get started in this book, from
the building blocks at your disposal to helpful tips for completing
your first build.

Let's get started!

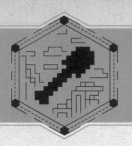

WHAT IS CREATIVE MODE?

WHY PLAY CREATIVE MODE?

1 FREE FLYING
Creative mode gives you the freedom of movement envied by all Survival players. To fly, double tap the jump key and use the jump and crouch keys to move higher or lower.

2 INSTANT MINING
You can break any block with one tap – even indestructible blocks. Instant mining is a huge time-saver and will allow you to create faster than ever.

3 PASSIVE MOBS
Hostile mobs are passive in Creative mode, so you don't have to fend them off or worry about pesky creepers destroying your work.

4 NO HUNGER
No health or hunger bars means you don't have to worry about eating food or skipping sleep.

Playing in Creative allows players to freely build constructions with an infinite supply of blocks and items, and lets players quickly remove or change blocks as they go. The mode removes survival aspects of the game, like hunger and damage, so you can have endless creative fun.

CREATIVE INVENTORY

The Creative inventory provides you with unlimited access to all the blocks in the game. Use the search bar to find a specific block or navigate via the nine helpful block tabs.

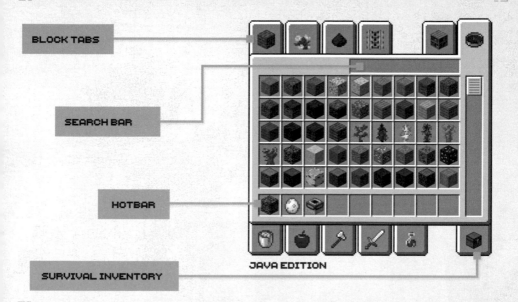

BLOCK TABS

SEARCH BAR

HOTBAR

JAVA EDITION

SURVIVAL INVENTORY

EXCLUSIVE CREATIVE MODE BLOCKS AND ITEMS

Some blocks are exclusive to Creative mode. It's impossible to create these in Survival mode! These include spawn eggs, End portal frames and more.

SPAWN EGGS

Use these eggs to spawn any mob you like!

END PORTAL FRAME

Create your very own gateway to the End.

BEST PRACTICES

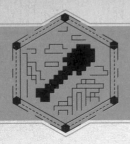

STAGE 1: PLANNING

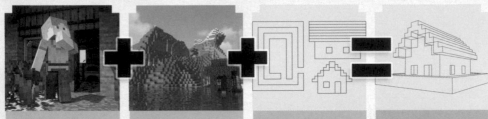

Pick what you want to build.

Decide where you want to build.

Sketch the outline for your build.

Your build schematics.

STAGE 2: STRUCTURE

Create an outline for your build.

Build the foundations.

Add in the build features.

Your build structure.

STAGE 3: DECORATING

Include the interior lighting.

Create some unique furniture.

Add decorative touches.

Your completed build.

Becoming an expert builder doesn't happen overnight. It takes practice, patience and planning. Splitting projects into simple, easy-to-follow stages will improve your creative work in no time! Follow these best practices to get started. Take your time and have fun with it!

THE COMMON PITFALLS

Making mistakes and starting over is all part of the game – a masterpiece takes time! Watch out for these common pitfalls that trip up beginners.

Keep your projects to a manageable size. Start small and work toward bigger builds.

Simple is best! A three-block color palette can look great.

Stick to your original idea. Don't change halfway through construction!

TOP TIP

The number one best practice is to back up your work. If you have an idea but you're not sure it will work, create a backup so you can start again if you make a mistake. Go to the menu, select the world, click edit and find the option "Copy World."

Although it's tempting, try to resist the allure of TNT. It's a fun, fast way to undo all your work.

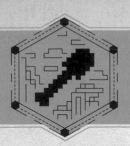

TYPES OF BLOCKS

CORE BLOCKS

The core blocks are the most common blocks in Minecraft and are primarily used as building blocks. There are three types of core block: basic, refined and shaped.

BASIC

These are the simplest blocks available to choose from. They generate naturally and can be found in biomes throughout Minecraft.

REFINED

Many of the basic blocks can be refined into similar variants, such as chiseled, smooth and mossy blocks. Refined blocks behave just like basic blocks, but with more detailed textures.

SHAPED

Basic and refined blocks can be crafted into shaped blocks, like stairs, slabs and walls. These shapes are used to add detail to builds.

There are over 600 unique blocks in Minecraft, from wood planks and stone bricks to copper stairs and redstone repeaters. That's a lot of blocks to play with! Luckily, they can be split into four main categories. Let's take a look at the various block types.

SPECIAL BLOCKS

In addition to your core blocks, there are also a number of blocks with special functions. These can be split into three categories: interactive, redstone and trigger.

INTERACTIVE BLOCKS

Interactive blocks perform an action when activated. Each interactive block has a unique function: e.g., doors will open and close, pistons will push and pull. Place these blocks in-game to find out more about their functions.

REDSTONE BLOCKS

Redstone blocks are used to create circuits and mechanisms. Each redstone block has a special function and can be used to create unique builds. Redstone can be challenging, so start simple and test the blocks out before you build your own circuit.

TRIGGER BLOCKS

Trigger blocks will activate interactive and redstone blocks. They are crucial for controlling redstone mechanisms. Trigger blocks are very useful for activating blocks such as lights and doors. Common trigger blocks are levers and buttons.

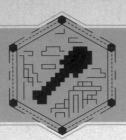

KNOW YOUR BLOCKS

ANCIENT EGYPTIAN

- Sandstone
- White wool
- Smooth quartz
- Glazed terracotta
- Acacia fences

- Jungle planks
- Dark oak slabs
- Campfires
- Spruce trapdoors
- Spruce planks

WILD WEST

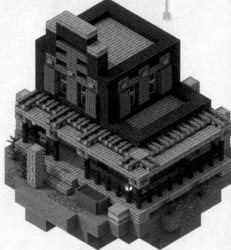

INFERNAL THEME

- Polished basalt
- Polished blackstone
- Magma
- Netherrack
- Weeping vines

Themes are a great way to make your build stand out. By combining carefully selected blocks you can create your very own personalized themes. If you're looking for inspiration, check out the themes below. Each of these themes focuses on five blocks to achieve the desired effects.

STEAMPUNK

- Dark prismarine
- Spruce planks
- Stone bricks
- White concrete
- Spruce wood

- Oak stairs
- Oak trapdoor
- Mossy cobblestone
- Cobblestone
- Spruce trees

WOODLAND

INDUSTRIAL

- Iron blocks
- Iron bars
- Polished andesite slabs
- Stone bricks
- Andesite

CHOOSE YOUR BLOCKS

SIMPLE COLORS

The simplest color schemes are made using two to three adjacent blocks on the color chart. These blocks can even be variations of the same color. This is known as an analogue color scheme.

COMPLEMENTARY COLORS

Choosing blocks that are directly opposite in color will create a color scheme that contrasts sharply while still looking good together. See below for complementary colors, like orange and turquoise.

Knowing how to pick the right blocks for your theme is a skill: the blocks you choose will define the look and character of your build. Before starting a new project, take a moment to select the base blocks that support your theme. Check out the color schemes below to get started!

FULL COLOR PALETTE

Larger builds typically use several colors to build character. Create a color palette by selecting several blocks that are equally spaced on the color graph. This will give your build wider variety and interest.

TEXTURE VARIANTS

Finally, you can add blocks to any color scheme by including variants. Simply decide on a color scheme and add blocks with multiple textures. Texture variants are great for avoiding uniform builds.

COMPLEMENTARY

EXPLORING THEMES WITH:
JERACRAFT

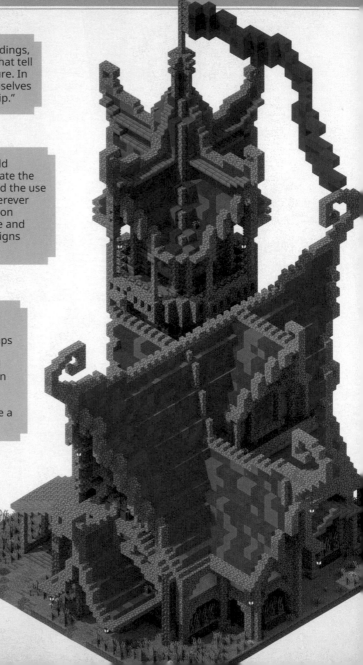

"When I think of elven buildings, I imagine the tales of old that tell of their connection to nature. In my mind, Elves pride themselves on a timeless craftsmanship."

"I wanted to make this build special, so I decided to create the modern elf home. I avoided the use of any wooden blocks, wherever possible, focusing instead on cobblestone, clay, concrete and wool to create flowing designs from the natural world."

"Once the building's frame was constructed using cobblestone, I filled the gaps using a variety of colorful blocks, before adding final details using a combination of stair blocks and slab blocks, with soul lanterns and chains added to create a sense of fantasy."

"This style of stone architecture gave me the freedom to create a natural build that blends into the landscape using organic shapes, plants and custom-made trees."

Having impressed millions of fans with his themed builds on YouTube, we asked master builder Jeracraft to talk to us about his creative process. Jeracraft has shared his modern elven building, which he describes as inspired by "elaborate flowing designs pulled from the natural world."

Using stair blocks in the roofs give the stonework a rugged, natural feel.

This modern house has been taken out of the wilderness and adapted to suit a metropolitan environment. The elaborate, flowing designs of the roofs and arches are to invoke the elven style.

Although this is a modern elven home, it still needed an intrinsic naturalistic feel to it. If you look closely, you'll see plants and mossy blocks thoughout the build.

While the build focuses on five main blocks, there are also several block variations used in the walls as well as the roof.

LIGHTING & EFFECTS

LIGHT LEVELS

There are 15 light levels in Minecraft and they come from a variety of light sources. Lighting will illuminate and showcase your build, and light level 8 is needed to prevent mobs from spawning, so proper use of lighting is essential.

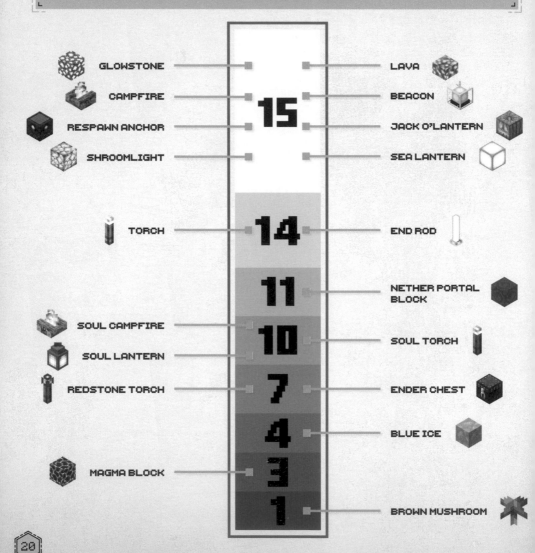

GLOWSTONE

CAMPFIRE

RESPAWN ANCHOR

SHROOMLIGHT

LAVA

BEACON

JACK O'LANTERN

SEA LANTERN

15

TORCH — **14** — END ROD

11 — NETHER PORTAL BLOCK

SOUL CAMPFIRE — **10** — SOUL TORCH

SOUL LANTERN

REDSTONE TORCH — **7** — ENDER CHEST

4 — BLUE ICE

MAGMA BLOCK — **3**

1 — BROWN MUSHROOM

Lighting is an essential element of all projects, and can mark the difference between a mediocre build and an epic one. How to use lighting is one of the biggest learning curves when playing Minecraft, so we've provided a key with all the information you need to master it.

LIGHTING EFFECTS

There are lots of ways to create lighting effects in Minecraft. Achieving the right lighting effect can be tricky, so here are some top tips to get you started.

DISCREET LIGHTING

Some lights don't need to be seen. Light will pass through transparent blocks like carpets, banners and paintings. Use this trick to light up your base with lights hidden in the walls and floors.

VARYING LEVELS

Use light levels to highlight certain features of your build. Each light level can add another layer of depth: the dim magma blocks and bright End rods work nicely to separate structure and biome.

DAYLIGHT DETECTORS

Some builds look great during the day and only need a little extra light at night. Use daylight detectors to automatically light up your base when the sun goes down, so it always looks the way you like it.

UNDERWATER LIGHTING

Using underwater lighting can have appealing results. Sea pickles are excellent for doing this: the more sea pickles you place (up to a maximum of four), the brighter the light they emit.

MOOD SETTING

Interior lighting that complements the room can have spectacular results. There are countless ways to use light creatively: Start by picking a light-emitting block and then think of clever ways to turn it into a feature for your build.

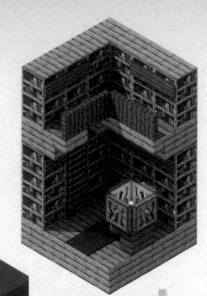

CANDLE HOLDER

Torches are the simplest kind of lighting and are very versatile. This library is illuminated by a candle holder composed of warped trapdoors, a torch and oak stairs.

AQUARIUM

Underwater lighting can be very appealing, but fitting it in can be difficult. Sea pickles need to be immersed in water to emit light, making them perfect for aquariums.

FIREPLACE

Make a fireplace by combining a campfire, iron bars and bricks. Campfires will burn indefinitely once lit.

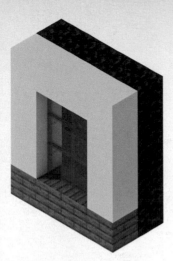

STAINED GLASS WINDOWS

Put a color tint on the view outside your windows by using stained glass. There are sixteen colors to choose from.

SCONCE

This light fixture is a fan favorite. Using an item frame, a slab and a torch, placed in that order, you can create this medieval looking sconce.

CHANDELIER

Create a fancy-looking chandelier by attaching End rods to a fence structure.

FIREWALL

Create a wall of lava by enclosing lava sources behind glass panes and stone blocks. Avoid using wooden blocks or they will catch fire and burn down!

SPOTLIGHT

Glowstone gives off the brightest light possible. This makes it perfect for a spotlight to showcase your coolest stuff, be it fun banners or enchanted equipment.

OUTDOOR SPACES

Lighting large outdoor space can be very tricky: Too much of the same light source can look dull, whereas mobs will start to spawn if there isn't enough light. There are lots of ways to light up outside space; simply pick a light source and see what you can create.

LAMPPOST

This lamppost has a hidden jack o'lantern to provide greater illumination. Check the chart on page 20 to see light levels.

COOKING CAULDRON

Build a campfire and place a cauldron on top of it for your own cooking pot. Why not add wooden benches and create a campsite?

SIGNAL BEACON

Signal beacons are ideal for illuminating large outdoor spaces as they can be placed wherever you want extra light.

FLUORESCENT SPIRES

A light source not to be overlooked is the End rod. These fluorescent rods are perfectly suited to modern-looking builds, like this spire!

PUMPKIN PATCH

These scary jack o'lantern pumpkins are the perfect subtle lighting. They're very bright, and if placed facing a wall, will act as a hidden light.

HAUNTED TREE

This large haunted tree glows with blue light from the soul torches on its branches. You can use as many torches as you like, making this suitable for both dim and bright lighting.

ETHEREAL POND

This mystical pond shimmers with light from sea pickles. These are perfect for adding a little fantasy to your build.

HANGING BASKET

Shroomlights are versatile lighting blocks. This hanging basket emits level 15 light and can happily fit into tight spaces.

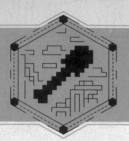

BIOMES & SUB-BIOMES

ICY IGLOO FORT

SNOWY TUNDRA

Bright white snow and minimal wildlife make snowy biomes ideal for winter-themed builds.

SUB-BIOME:
Snowy mountains

FARMING VILLAGE

PLAINS

This flat, grassy biome is full of open space and water, making it ideal for large, open builds such as farms.

SUB-BIOME:
Sunflower plains

Where you choose to build is just as important as the project itself. There are many unique biomes across the Overworld, the Nether and the End, and it's up to you to find the biome that best suits your ideas. Jump into Creative mode and fly around to see which ones you can discover.

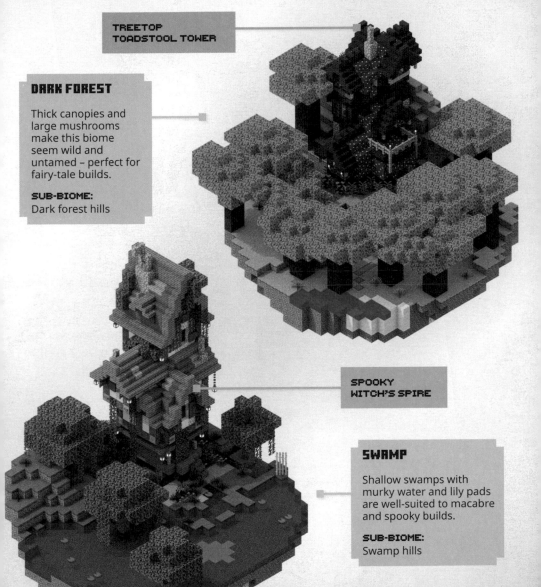

TREETOP TOADSTOOL TOWER

DARK FOREST

Thick canopies and large mushrooms make this biome seem wild and untamed – perfect for fairy-tale builds.

SUB-BIOME: Dark forest hills

SPOOKY WITCH'S SPIRE

SWAMP

Shallow swamps with murky water and lily pads are well-suited to macabre and spooky builds.

SUB-BIOME: Swamp hills

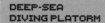

DEEP-SEA DIVING PLATORM

OCEAN

Ocean biomes are ideal for floating homes and underwater builds.

SUB-BIOME:
Warm ocean

NEW FRONTIER CASTLE

WARPED FOREST

This dark turquoise Nether biome is full of coves and hideaways – perfect for fantastical builds.

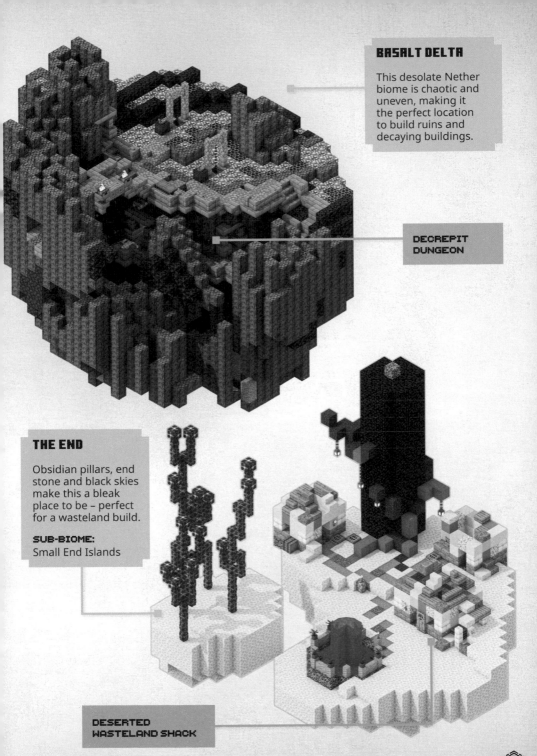

BASALT DELTA

This desolate Nether biome is chaotic and uneven, making it the perfect location to build ruins and decaying buildings.

DECREPIT DUNGEON

THE END

Obsidian pillars, end stone and black skies make this a bleak place to be – perfect for a wasteland build.

SUB-BIOME:
Small End Islands

DESERTED WASTELAND SHACK

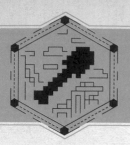

TERRAFORMING LANDSCAPES

TERRAFORMING FOR BEGINNERS

There are no *rules* to terraforming. Everyone works in their own way, and any changes you make will count as terraforming. That said, here are some top tips to help you get started.

1 SCOUT A SITE

Search the surrounding area for a biome that fits your needs. Using an existing biome with a desired feature, like a mountain or a generated structure, could save you hours of terraforming time.

2 PICK A THEME

Choose blocks that support your theme and location. These could be new blocks or those already present in the biome. Using variants of existing blocks is a great way to add character.

3 START SIMPLE

Start with a small test area: Remove the blocks you don't want and place some that you do. Try to re-create natural features like rivers and fields to test your abilities.

BEFORE

If you can't find a suitable biome, consider terraforming. If you've ever carved a room out of a mountainside or cleared a field of trees, then you've tried your hand at it already. Terraforming is when you intentionally reshape a landscape, and is an important skill for builders.

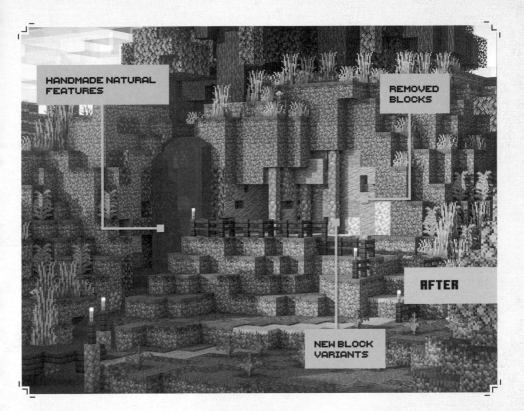

HANDMADE NATURAL FEATURES

REMOVED BLOCKS

AFTER

NEW BLOCK VARIANTS

4 VIEW FROM AFAR

Once you have completed your test area, take a moment to view your work from afar. Does it look like you imagined? Should you reconsider your block choices? Take the time you need to ensure it's exactly what you want.

5 COMPLETE YOUR WORK

Once you're happy with your test area, start expanding your work to fit the area you need. Work slowly and methodically, and remember to check your work every now and then to ensure you achieve your desired effect.

TOP TIP

There's no limit to what you can terraform in Minecraft. Most players focus on small structures, while some will go so far as to create entire biomes. You can terraform everything you see around you.

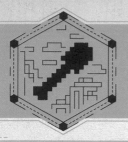

CREATIVE COMMANDS

LOCATE

The locate tool will give you the nearest coordinates of generated structures. Use the command

```
/locate village
```

LOCATE BIOME (JAVA EDITION)

The locate biome tool will give you the coordinates of any biome type. Use the command

```
/locatebiome minecraft :beach
```

TELEPORT

The teleport command will send you to any set of coordinates. This is useful with the locate command. Use the command

```
/tp player 10 10 10
```

TIME

You can control the time of day. If you have a preference for building during the day or late at night, use the command

```
/time set day
```

WEATHER

You can also control the weather. If you want to see your build in the rain or during the sunshine, use the command

```
/weather rain
```

Playing in Creative mode gives you access to the in-game commands. These commands are very helpful, and using them properly will be a key timesaver when you're starting a new build. They're so helpful that using these in Survival mode counts as cheating!

GAME MODE

Want to test out your build in another game mode? Use the command

`/gamemode creative`

INVENTORY

You can control various rules using the gamerule command, like the keep inventory rule. Use the command

`/gamerule keepInventory`

GRIEFING

Worried about having your work undone by exploding creepers or block-stealing endermen? To change the settings, use the command

`/gamerule mobGriefing`

SEED (JAVA EDITION)

If you've found a world you enjoy and want to recreate it, use the command below. Bedrock players can find the seed on the world options menu.

`/seed`

COMMANDS

For a full list of available commands use

`/help`

CONSTRUCTION

Now that you're familiar with the blocks and biomes, it's time to
look at how we can use them. In this block-filled game, being able
to identify the shapes used in construction will quickly make you
a construction expert. But there's more to building than just
construction! An expert builder is also an inspired decorator.
Let's take a look at what these shapes and decorations are.

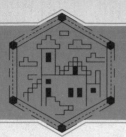

SHAPES

For many builders, simplicity is key. Understanding basic shapes and how they can be used together will give you the ability to create anything. Let's take a look at what these basic shapes are.

TRIANGULAR PRISMS

Triangular shapes can be used for roofing, walls and even as bases. The slanted angles add character and complexity to structures.

CUBOIDS

Square and rectangular cuboids are the most commonly used shapes due to their simplicity. They are often used for short-term bases, quick builds and simple structures.

PYRAMIDS

Pyramids are iconic construction shapes. They are ideal for roofing and even as a structure on their own.

Every structure in Minecraft, no matter how grand or complicated, can be simplified into basic shapes. When building a new structure, try breaking it down into its core components before starting. Understanding how shapes work together will help you analyze any build.

SPHERES

Although it is impossible to create a perfect circle in Minecraft, you can create similar shapes. Spheres are made using a series of these circular shapes. They're very popular in this block-filled world.

CYLINDERS

Cylinders are an extension of the circular shapes used for spheres. This shape has more character and complexity than normal cuboid shapes, and can be used both vertically and horizonally.

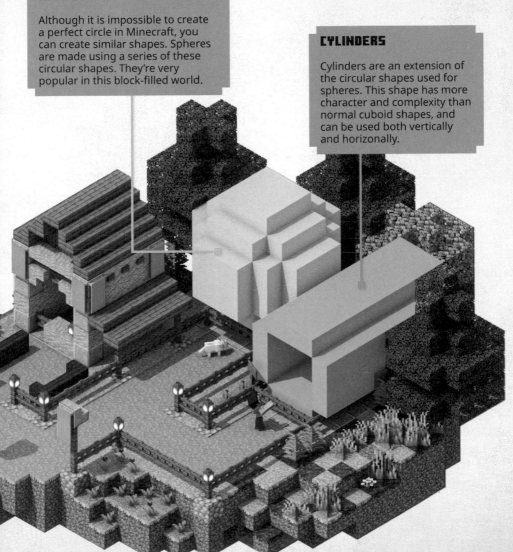

CUBOIDS: EXPLAINED

Cuboids are the most basic of shapes. A cuboid is any square or rectangular structure with four walls, and is often a beginner's first build. They are widely used in construction, and can be found in almost every large build.

CUBOIDS

Cuboids have six sides, two horizontal, two vertical and two lengthwise.

PYRAMIDS

PYRAMIDS: EXPLAINED

Pyramids are popular structure shapes. They are usually composed of four triangular sides atop a square base. Pyramids are versatile structures, offering a change from the usual block world. They're commonly used as roofs and even as builds themselves.

SQUARE BASE

The base will determine the size and shape of the pyramid. A square base with equal sides will create the perfect base of triangular walls.

TRIANGLES

Pyramids are composed of triangles. To create the triangles, remove a block on either side of each layer as you build from the base up.

SLOPES

To achieve the angled slope of the pyramid, place the blocks in a staircase formation, moving closer to the center on each level.

TRIANGULAR PRISMS: EXPLAINED

Triangular prisms are as popular as pyramids for building bases. The extended triangular shape works well both as roofing and as buildings, such as tents or barns. Although similar to pyramids, its more complicated and versatile shape makes it more popular among experienced builders.

TRIANGULAR ENDS

Just like a pyramid, the two smaller ends are shaped like triangles. To create the triangle, simply remove a block as you build each layer from the base up.

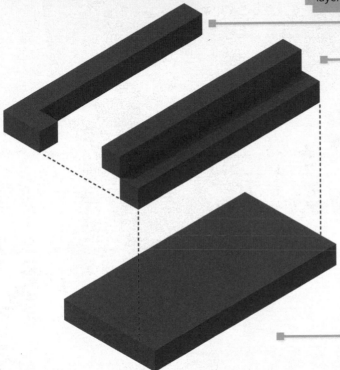

STAIRCASE SIDES

The sides are built like a staircase, moving 1 block toward the center as you go up each level.

RECTANGULAR BASE

Prisms are typically set on a rectangular base. It can be any length you like, but the height will be determined by its width.

THESE ARE ALL TRIANGULAR PRISMS!

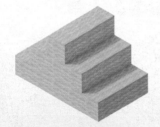

SHORT

ANGLE

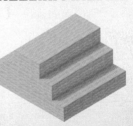

WIDE

SPHERES: EXPLAINED

Spheres are the most challenging shapes to create in Minecraft — but they don't have to be! Spheres are essentially a series of larger and smaller rings connected to each other. You can create a dome by only building half of the shape.

SMALLER CIRCLES

Now build 4 circles, each smaller than the last: 9x9, 9x9, 7x7, 5x5.

BIGGER CIRCLES

Build 3 more circles, each larger than the last: 7x7, 9x9, 9x9. The first 9x9 circle has a 1-block edge on the top and sides. The second has a 3-block edge.

ANOTHER CIRCLE

Build another 9x9 circle. This one has a 5-block edge.

FIRST CIRCLE

Start by creating a 5x5 circle using the outlines as a guide.

THESE ARE ALL SPHERICAL BUILDS!

LARGE

SMALL

DOME

ELLIPSOID

CYLINDER: EXPLAINED

Cylinders are another key structure in Minecraft. They are a mix between cuboids and spheres and are a great shape for constructing spacious and detailed builds.

CIRCULAR BASE

Start by creating a 7x7 circular base using the outline as a guide. You can create smaller and larger cylinders by adding or removing 2x2 blocks: 9x9, 13x13, 15x15.

CIRCULAR WALLS

Using the base outline, extend the walls to be an equal height to the outline: Using the 7x7 base, extend the walls 8 blocks tall.

HORIZONTAL AND VERTICAL

Cylinders can be built both vertically and horizontally. To build a horizontal cylinder, follow the instructions on this page starting with a vertical base.

THESE ARE BOTH CYLINDRICAL BUILDS!

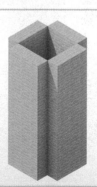

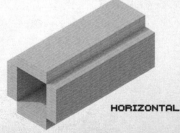

VERTICAL

HORIZONTAL

BLOCK HACKS: INTERIORS

DINING CHAIR

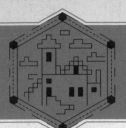

Use trapdoors and stair blocks to create chairs. Banners also make great cushions.

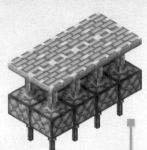

PISTON TABLE

Activated pistons protrude from redstone torches with table-like legs. Perfect for dining rooms.

STAIRCASE

Spiral staircases are space-efficient and look great.

FIREPLACE

Fireplaces can be packed with detail. Fill the mantelpiece with decor and guard the fire with rails.

Once you've completed your build, it's time to decorate! There are many decorative blocks available in-game to choose from, but you can also combine blocks to make unique features. Take inspiration from the world around you and see what furnishings you can create.

INFINITY SHOWER

Glass panes and prismarine are perfect for showers. Place a hidden water source overhead for a dripping water effect.

BATHTUB

Ready for a long soak? Bathtubs are great for waiting out the night.

SHARED SINKS

Cauldrons can double as sinks. The white light-emitting End rods are the ideal light source for bathrooms.

WINDOWS

Be sure to include glass pane windows to take advantage of the daylight. Banner curtains and a windowsill will make your base look more complete.

SHELVING

Shelves are a great way to fill up empty walls. You can store plants, chests or even put your best items on display.

LOUNGE AREA

A lounge area is incomplete without a sofa! Use stairs for the sofa and slabs for a coffee table.

KITCHEN

Cauldrons also make for great kitchen sinks. Use a trapdoor to make it look like a cabinet.

DINING TABLE

Sometimes you only need a simple table and chairs. This table is made with slabs and carpets, and the chairs are made with stairs and signs.

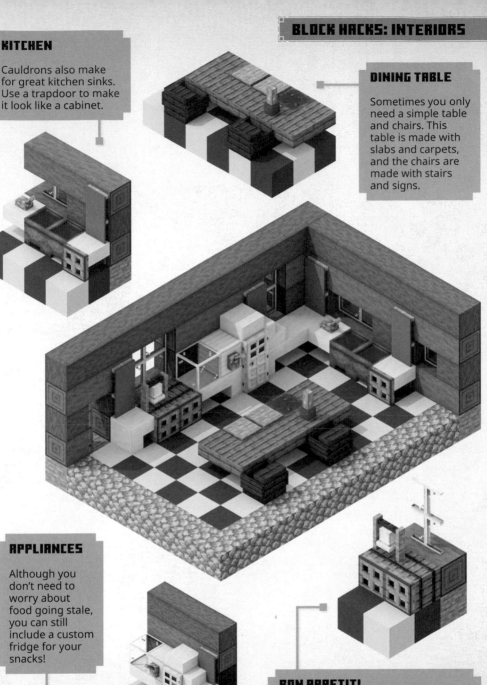

APPLIANCES

Although you don't need to worry about food going stale, you can still include a custom fridge for your snacks!

BON APPETIT!

A town bell can be heard from far away – perfect for summoning your friends for a meal.

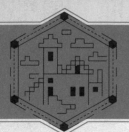

PLANTERS

This windowsill planter is made using dirt and trapdoors. Plants like poppies and tulips will fill the space with color.

SHUTTERS

Shutters are a fantastic, realistic addition to any window. Trapdoors are suitable for this as they can be placed on most surfaces.

ROOFING

Making a roof look exciting can be challenging. Adding small details like buttons and signs is a great place to start.

CHIMNEY SMOKE

An active chimney is a sign of life. This chimney uses cobwebs to give a permanent illusion of smoke.

A build is not complete until the exterior is as well decorated as the interior! There are countless ways you can do this, like outdoor furniture and shrubbery. Use your imagination and pick decorations that work with your theme. What will you build?

VARIANTS

Uniform walls can look dull. You can incorporate some block variants to give them more character.

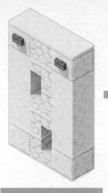

TRELLIS

Trellises are great for filling large spaces. They can be used to add lighting and greenery too.

UNIQUE DECOR

Why not add some quirky features to the walls, such as this ball and chain. It may not be functional but it sure looks good.

BALCONY

Build some extra outdoor space. This balcony is perfect for a desert biome.

BRIDGES

Although simple and quick to build, bridges add a lot to the outdoor decor.

WATERING HOLE

In places far from rivers and oceans, watering holes are essential. This hole has created an infinite water supply by lining 3 water sources side-by-side. Don't try this in the Nether or your water will evaporate!

NETHER PLANTER

Combine the crimson red and warped blue hues of the Nether to create mood-setting structures, like this fungi planter.

STAINED GLASS WINDOW

Consider using stained glass for your thematic builds. This Nether-inspired build uses gray stained glass.

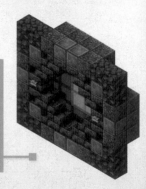

CRANE

Another non-functional decor, it's extra details like this crane that help make a build stand out. The contrast against the quartz highlights the texture differences.

GRAND WALKWAY

An impressive build deserves an impressive walkway. This tiered version has a simple but elegant design.

POTTED ARCH

Instead of complete walls, try using some arches. They help open out the space, and you can add extra greenery to spruce up your build.

USING SHAPES WITH:
WATTLES

"Whenever I begin a new build, I start with a basic shape and then I slowly add more. This elite Roman-themed temple comprises 4 shapes: the entrance is a rectangle, the main shape of the temple is a circle, the temple room itself is a square, and then on top sits a dome!"

"To create more advanced builds like this, try starting with just the outlines of the shapes. Then use trial and error, and lots of it, to get the final structure you want."

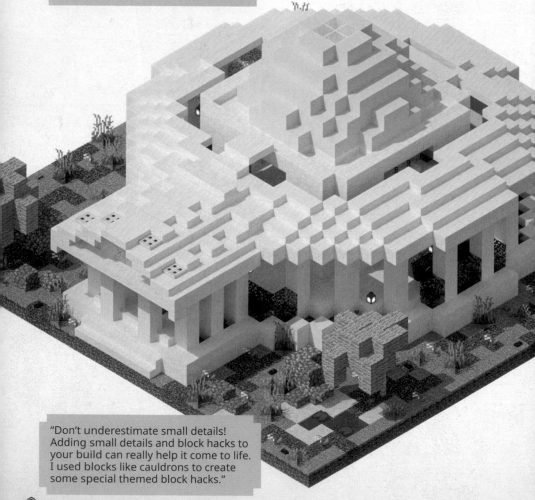

"Don't underestimate small details! Adding small details and block hacks to your build can really help it come to life. I used blocks like cauldrons to create some special themed block hacks."

Even the most complex builds – like this elite Roman-themed temple – have to start somewhere, and it can be a little daunting solving how to get from basic shapes to advanced creations. Lucky for you, YouTuber and master builder Wattles is here to give you some top tips.

"Cauldrons look cool. Hanging a few chains from the ceiling with cauldrons directly below will make a hanging bucket."

"Campfires are great for adding light. Place a campfire on top of a block. Put signs all the way around the campfire to create a box."

You can keep making changes until the build is finished. "Although I started with basic shapes, I still wanted the temple to be open-air. I removed blocks from the walls and ceilings to open the build up."

"Did you know that you can place an open trapdoor against a wall, fence or iron bar and they'll connect? This is a great way to finish walls."

CONSTRUCTION COMBOS

EXTRA SPACE

This build combines two basic shapes to create a house: a cuboid and a triangular prism. A second prism has been added to the roof as an alcove for additional space.

EFFECTS

Using cobwebs as chimney smoke is a fun block hack for creating unique chimneys.

THEME

Blocks have been carefully selected for a woodland theme. Using a mix of core blocks, like stairs, walls and slabs, has had a wonderful tiering effect on the final build.

EXTERIORS

A few finishing touches to the exterior help make the build feel complete.

Now that you know your blocks, themes, shapes and block hacks, it's time to look at how they can be used together. Learn to combine each of these and you'll soon be creating any structure imaginable. These can be simple affixed structures or more complicated merged together.

MERGED

You can get more creative with how you join two structures. Overlapping shapes will create some fun and unique shapes. This is an easy skill to learn with a little practice, and once you've mastered it, your only limitation is your imagination.

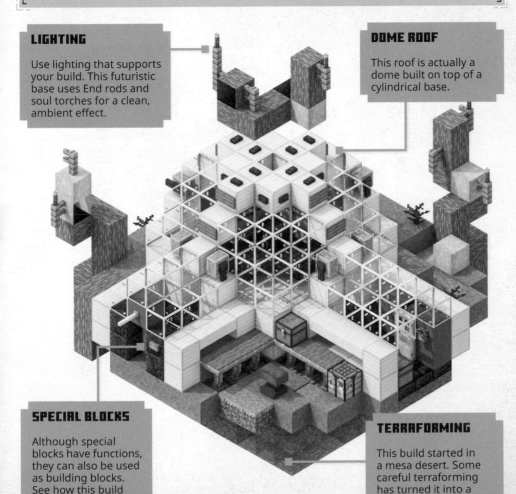

LIGHTING

Use lighting that supports your build. This futuristic base uses End rods and soul torches for a clean, ambient effect.

DOME ROOF

This roof is actually a dome built on top of a cylindrical base.

SPECIAL BLOCKS

Although special blocks have functions, they can also be used as building blocks. See how this build uses anvils, buttons and pistons.

TERRAFORMING

This build started in a mesa desert. Some careful terraforming has turned it into a unique biome.

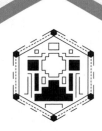

BUILDS

Finding inspiration and getting started can be tricky for budding Minecrafters, so we've included a selection of unique structures for you to build in-game. Follow the instructions on the following pages to complete the builds. Can you spot any of the techniques we've covered so far?

Feel free to personalize these builds and make them your own!

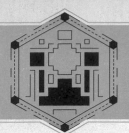

GLORIOUS GREENHOUSE

MAIN BLOCKS

FRONT

SIDE

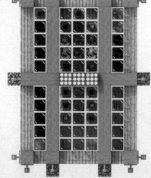

TOP

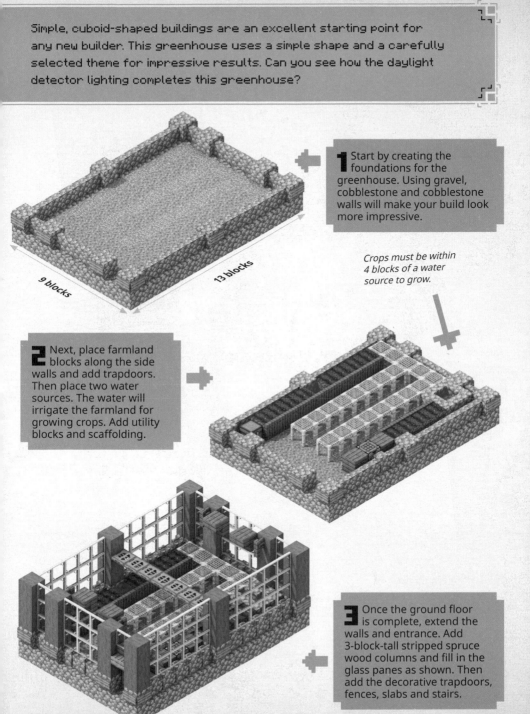

Simple, cuboid-shaped buildings are an excellent starting point for any new builder. This greenhouse uses a simple shape and a carefully selected theme for impressive results. Can you see how the daylight detector lighting completes this greenhouse?

1 Start by creating the foundations for the greenhouse. Using gravel, cobblestone and cobblestone walls will make your build look more impressive.

Crops must be within 4 blocks of a water source to grow.

9 blocks

13 blocks

2 Next, place farmland blocks along the side walls and add trapdoors. Then place two water sources. The water will irrigate the farmland for growing crops. Add utility blocks and scaffolding.

3 Once the ground floor is complete, extend the walls and entrance. Add 3-block-tall stripped spruce wood columns and fill in the glass panes as shown. Then add the decorative trapdoors, fences, slabs and stairs.

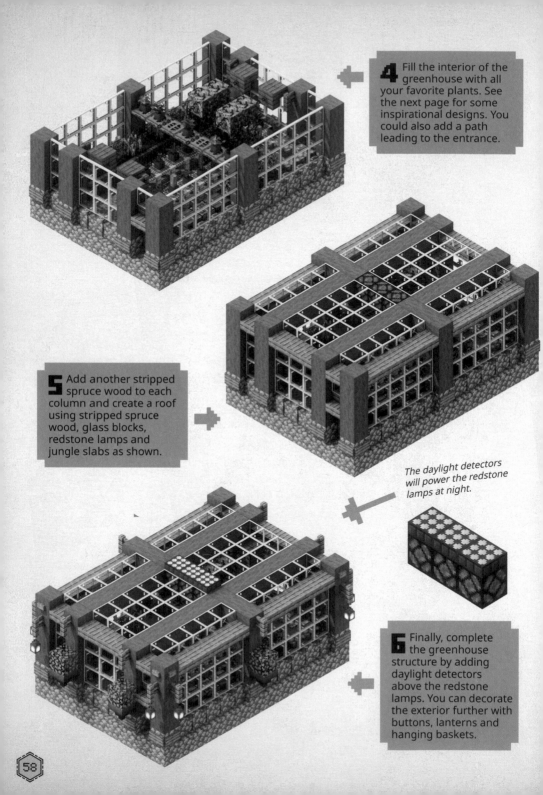

4 Fill the interior of the greenhouse with all your favorite plants. See the next page for some inspirational designs. You could also add a path leading to the entrance.

5 Add another stripped spruce wood to each column and create a roof using stripped spruce wood, glass blocks, redstone lamps and jungle slabs as shown.

The daylight detectors will power the redstone lamps at night.

6 Finally, complete the greenhouse structure by adding daylight detectors above the redstone lamps. You can decorate the exterior further with buttons, lanterns and hanging baskets.

HANGING GARDENS

Use leaves and vines to create an overgrown nature effect!

BENCHES

Fill the benches with potted plants. Scaffolding makes for great greenhouse benches!

WORKBENCH

Be sure to include a crafting table nearby. They're handy to have around!

HANGING BASKET

Create your own hopper baskets to add greenery to the exterior of your build.

CROPS

Plant a variety of crops. Beetroot tastes delicious in soups.

OVERHEAD SHELVES

Take advantage of the overhead storage. These shelves hold more plant pots.

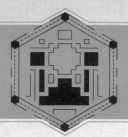

ENCHANTED FOREST COTTAGE

DIFFICULTY:

⬚⬚⬚⬚⬚

🕑 60 mins

MAIN BLOCKS

FRONT

SIDE

TOP

Choosing the best biome to suit your build can make a big difference. This build has an enchanted forest theme, and what biome is more magical than a warped forest? Before starting the build, take a moment to see if you can identify each of the basic shapes used to complete the cottage.

1 Start by locating a suitable warped forest and create the foundations for the cottage. You can prepare designated areas, like a kitchen, by using different blocks and patterns.

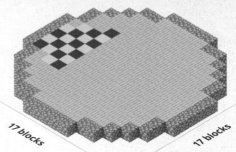

17 blocks

17 blocks

2 Begin building the walls around the edges of the of the foundation, leaving space for a dark oak door and three glass pane windows. Use a mix of cobblestone and stone variants to give the walls character.

3 Add stripped birch wood to your block selection and continue building the cottage walls and windows. Then create a decorative lintel above the doorway using andesite, andesite stairs and a chiseled stone brick.

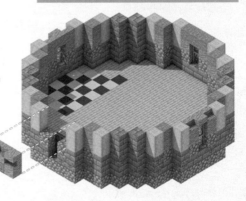

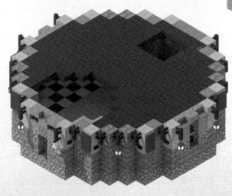

4 Next, build a dark oak platform using slabs, leaving two large gaps as shown. Then add lighting and decorative details to the exterior.

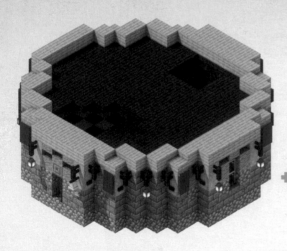

Using fences to hang lanterns and bells is a great way to add depth.

5 Start creating the outline of the cottage's roof. Use both birch planks and birch slabs to help give the roof a tiered effect.

6 Using birch slabs, create an awning around the building. The awning not only adds extra detail but is also perfect for your hanging lanterns and bell.

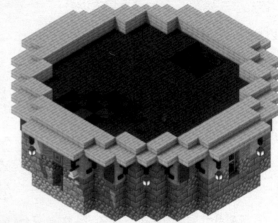

The upside-down stone brick stairs will help make the cottage feel more spacious.

7 Next, add new block types to contrast the cottage's birch roof. This build features hay bales and stone brick stairs as they stand out against the birch blocks – see pages 16-17 to find out more about picking blocks for themes.

8 Continue building the roof with another ring of blocks above those from step 7. This additional block height will give players the space they need to stand upright.

9 Add another ring of blocks, moving one block closer to the center to create a domed shape.

10 Add another ring of blocks, leaving a 5x5 gap in the center.

TOP TIP

The cottage's roof is shaped like a dome sectioned into four pieces. See pages 40-41 to learn more about spherical shapes and how to build them.

11 Seal the top of the roof with a skylight window. The skylight will fill the room with natural light during the day. Next, create alcoves on each side of your cottage using dark oak variants.

The blue hue of soul campfires makes the cottage feel enchanted.

12 Finally, add the finishing touches to the exterior. Place birch signs and buttons along the alcove walls to contrast with the dark oak and use soul campfires to light up the cottage.

TOP TIP

Adding side rooms and alcoves to builds is a great technique for making a build appear more spacious.

KITCHEN

Create a kitchen in the tiled gray and white concrete section of the ground floor. Include furnaces for cooking food and chests for storing it in.

GROUND FLOOR

BEDROOM

Place a bed on the second floor and use it to save your location. Include chests full of useful items so you're ready to get back in the action as soon as you respawn.

VINE STAIRWAY

This vine serves a dual purpose: a stairway to the next floor and as greenery. Plants can be great for creativity and are known to reduce stress!

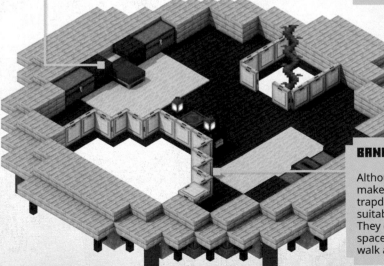

BANISTERS

Although fences make great barriers, trapdoors are more suitable as banisters. They occupy the same space but allow you to walk about freely.

SECOND FLOOR

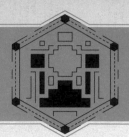

CORAL COVE HABITAT

DIFFICULTY:

🕐 50 mins

MAIN BLOCKS

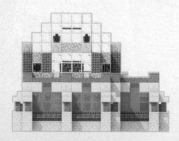

FRONT

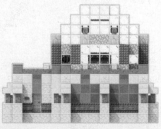

SIDE

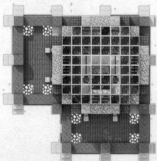

TOP

Building underwater comes with its own set of challenges, from breathing underwater to draining water out of rooms. Playing in Creative mode will make this easier, but it's always helpful to practice. Start by finding a colorful coral reef for your habitat and then start building.

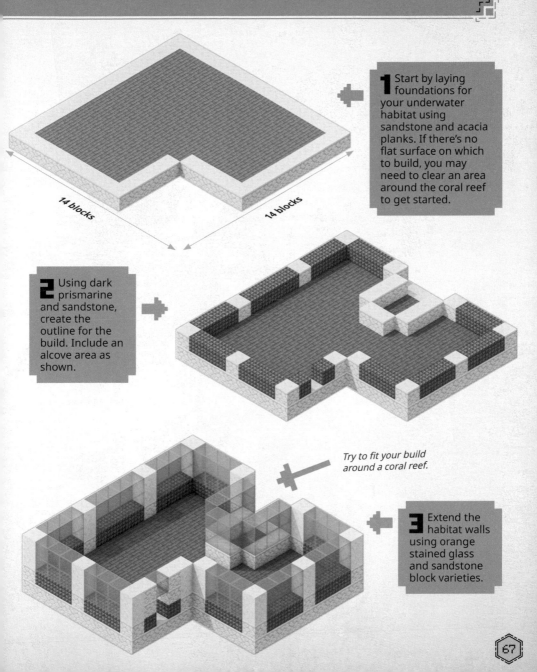

14 blocks

14 blocks

1 Start by laying foundations for your underwater habitat using sandstone and acacia planks. If there's no flat surface on which to build, you may need to clear an area around the coral reef to get started.

2 Using dark prismarine and sandstone, create the outline for the build. Include an alcove area as shown.

Try to fit your build around a coral reef.

3 Extend the habitat walls using orange stained glass and sandstone block varieties.

4 Spruce up the exterior with some fancy support columns using stairs, walls, blocks and signs. Place an iron door in the doorway and buttons to open and close it.

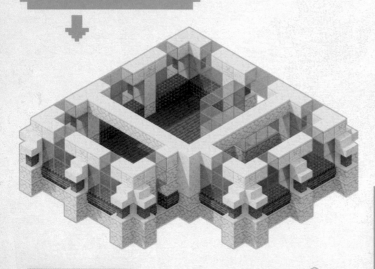

5 Extend the walls another block using the sandstone and orange stained glass. Then start adding another floor with two beams as shown.

6 Fill in the new floor using acacia slabs and glowstone. Leave a gap for a ladder. The glowstone will provide some mood-setting light.

TOP TIP

It can be very dark underwater. Use a Potion of Night Vision so you can see clearly.

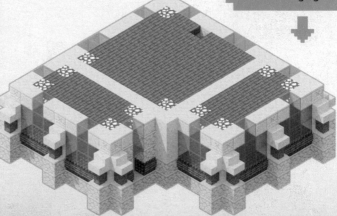

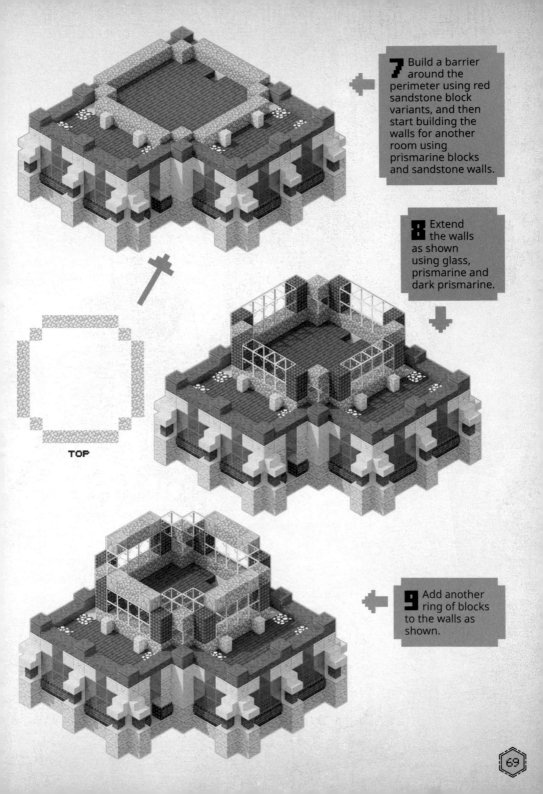

7 Build a barrier around the perimeter using red sandstone block variants, and then start building the walls for another room using prismarine blocks and sandstone walls.

8 Extend the walls as shown using glass, prismarine and dark prismarine.

TOP

9 Add another ring of blocks to the walls as shown.

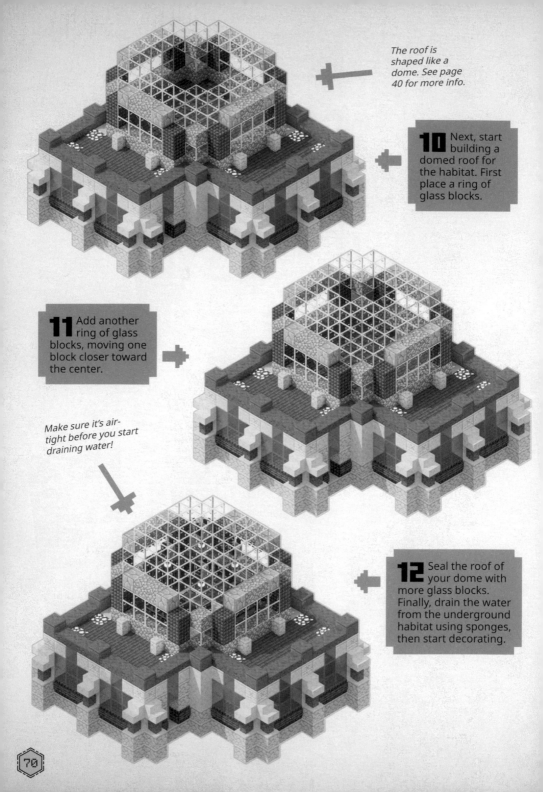

The roof is shaped like a dome. See page 40 for more info.

10 Next, start building a domed roof for the habitat. First place a ring of glass blocks.

11 Add another ring of glass blocks, moving one block closer toward the center.

Make sure it's air-tight before you start draining water!

12 Seal the roof of your dome with more glass blocks. Finally, drain the water from the underground habitat using sponges, then start decorating.

MULTI-STORY

Place ladders on the far wall to reach the second floor. Your build must be drained before you can place the ladders.

GROUND FLOOR

OVERHEAD LIGHTING

Remember to add lighting to your build. Overhead lighting is an effective way to add light sources without cluttering the build.

DESIGNATED AREAS

Create some designated areas with some creative block placement. The gray and white carpets make it clear this is the kitchen.

WINDOWS

The windows allow you to watch the ocean as you fall asleep. For a mood-setting ambience, consider using stained glass instead of regular glass.

SECOND FLOOR

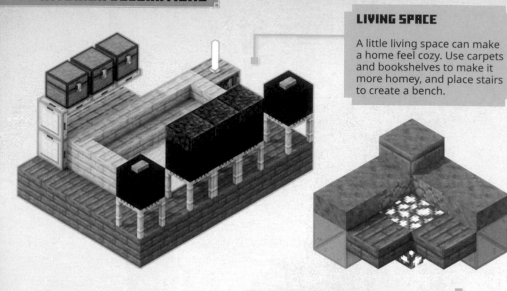

LIVING SPACE

A little living space can make a home feel cozy. Use carpets and bookshelves to make it more homey, and place stairs to create a bench.

TV STAND

Familiar decorations help make a build feel more final and complete. You can add features from your own home, like this TV stand made using scaffolding, buttons and blocks.

GLOWSTONE

Build simple lights directly into the structure with glowstone.

ENTRANCE

Include an airlock entrance for getting in and out of the habitat. Watch out you don't flood the ground floor!

MASTER BEDROOM

Fall asleep to the soothing light of the ocean above the dome. This large bedroom features windows on all sides for a panoramic view filled with ocean life.

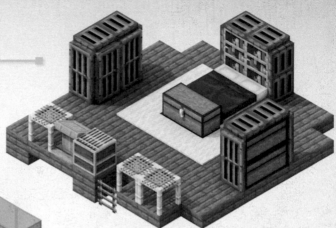

CORAL GARDEN

Fill your mini alcove with corals and add plenty of sea pickles to bring out all their wonderful colors.

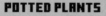

POTTED PLANTS

Use jungle trapdoors, dirt and ferns to create potted plants. These compact furnishings can fit in the smallest of spaces.

FLOORING

Carpets, like these black and white carpets, make for practical floor tiles. They provide an excellent visual contrast in the large open space.

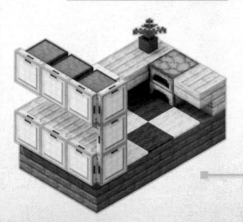

TRADE TRICKS WITH:
TEAM VISIONARY

When starting a new build, the first step is to pick a theme. This temple build has been styled on the beautiful temples of China, complete with the conical roof. "You'll notice we make use of a lot of slabs, stairs and even fence gates. These are small blocks that can make a striking difference in your build."

Once the theme is chosen, the next step is to create a block choice for the build. "We used various blocks, primarily TNT, birch logs and white terracotta, to pack the walls with color." Establishing the block choice early ensures the theme is the same from start to finish.

Before finishing the build, look and see if there are more small details you can add. Placing details "symmetrically around the build" – such as buttons and trapdoors – will leave a clean finish that looks good on all sides.

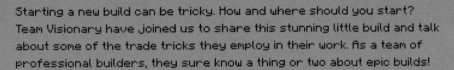

Starting a new build can be tricky. How and where should you start? Team Visionary have joined us to share this stunning little build and talk about some of the trade tricks they employ in their work. As a team of professional builders, they sure know a thing or two about epic builds!

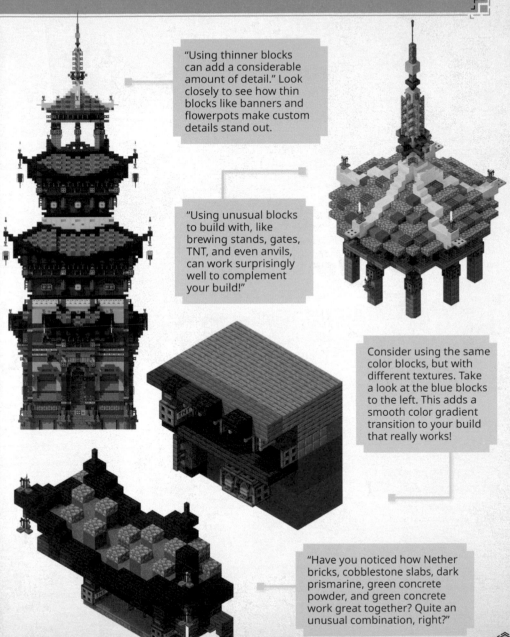

"Using thinner blocks can add a considerable amount of detail." Look closely to see how thin blocks like banners and flowerpots make custom details stand out.

"Using unusual blocks to build with, like brewing stands, gates, TNT, and even anvils, can work surprisingly well to complement your build!"

Consider using the same color blocks, but with different textures. Take a look at the blue blocks to the left. This adds a smooth color gradient transition to your build that really works!

"Have you noticed how Nether bricks, cobblestone slabs, dark prismarine, green concrete powder, and green concrete work great together? Quite an unusual combination, right?"

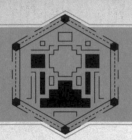

FUTURISTIC COMPOUND

DIFFICULTY:

◇◇◇◇◆

⏱ 90 mins

MAIN BLOCKS

FRONT

SIDE

TOP

You can improve your builds immensely with a little forward-planning. Building lighting into the structure foundations will hide the messy redstone mechanisms while creating impressive lights. This method of hiding redstone can be used for lots of different purposes.

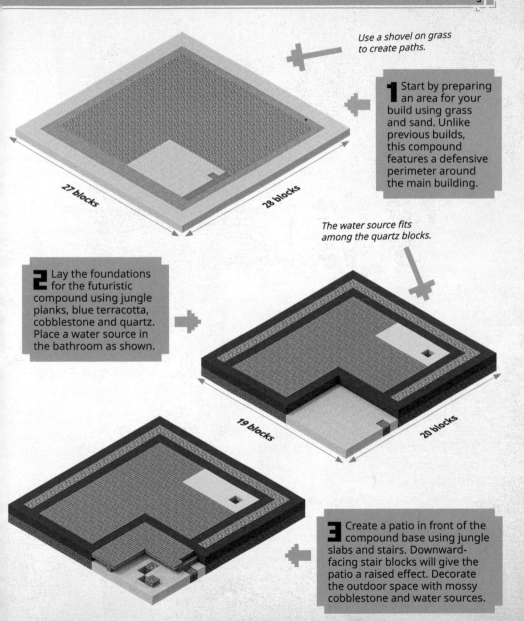

Use a shovel on grass to create paths.

1 Start by preparing an area for your build using grass and sand. Unlike previous builds, this compound features a defensive perimeter around the main building.

27 blocks

28 blocks

The water source fits among the quartz blocks.

2 Lay the foundations for the futuristic compound using jungle planks, blue terracotta, cobblestone and quartz. Place a water source in the bathroom as shown.

19 blocks

20 blocks

3 Create a patio in front of the compound base using jungle slabs and stairs. Downward-facing stair blocks will give the patio a raised effect. Decorate the outdoor space with mossy cobblestone and water sources.

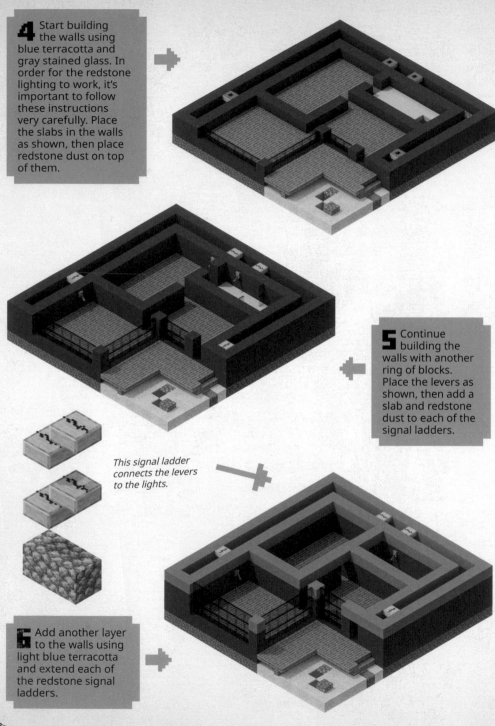

4 Start building the walls using blue terracotta and gray stained glass. In order for the redstone lighting to work, it's important to follow these instructions very carefully. Place the slabs in the walls as shown, then place redstone dust on top of them.

5 Continue building the walls with another ring of blocks. Place the levers as shown, then add a slab and redstone dust to each of the signal ladders.

This signal ladder connects the levers to the lights.

6 Add another layer to the walls using light blue terracotta and extend each of the redstone signal ladders.

7 Continue building the walls, using smooth quartz stairs atop the gray stained glass. Then add a final slab and redstone dust to each of the signal ladders.

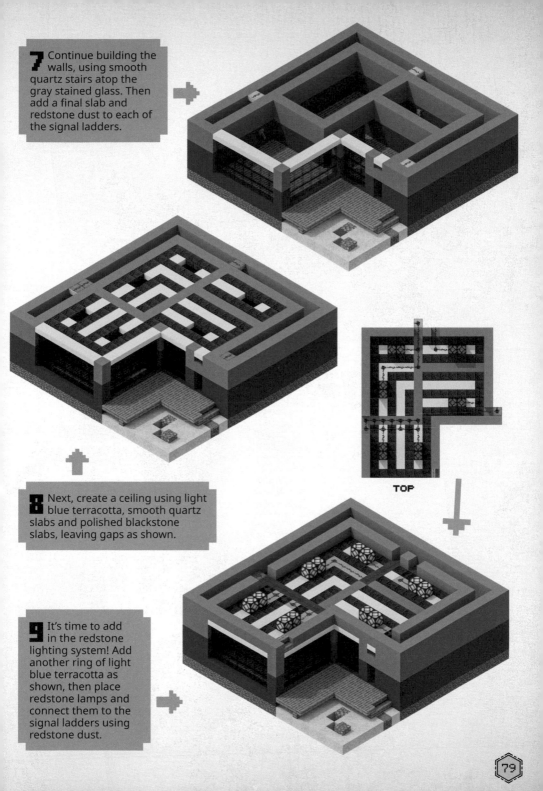

TOP

8 Next, create a ceiling using light blue terracotta, smooth quartz slabs and polished blackstone slabs, leaving gaps as shown.

9 It's time to add in the redstone lighting system! Add another ring of light blue terracotta as shown, then place redstone lamps and connect them to the signal ladders using redstone dust.

10 Next, hide the lighting system beneath a garden of grass and podzol. Build a jungle staircase leading to the roof and create a path leading through the garden.

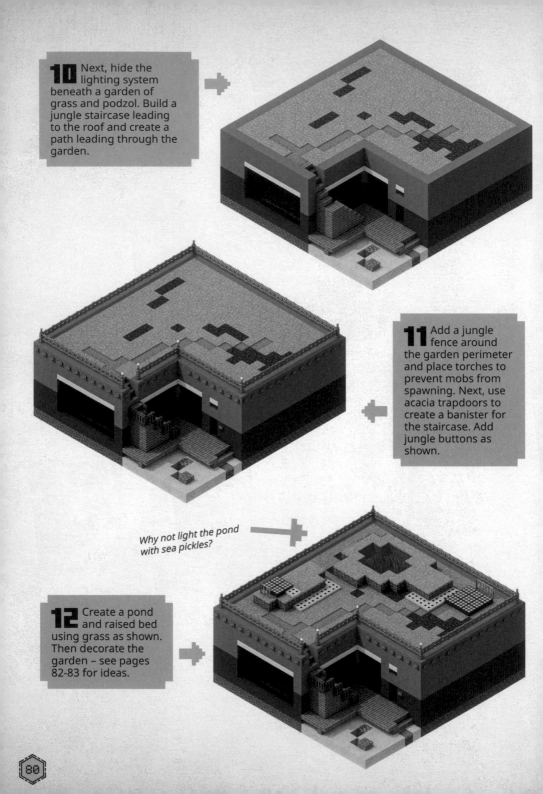

11 Add a jungle fence around the garden perimeter and place torches to prevent mobs from spawning. Next, use acacia trapdoors to create a banister for the staircase. Add jungle buttons as shown.

Why not light the pond with sea pickles?

12 Create a pond and raised bed using grass as shown. Then decorate the garden – see pages 82-83 for ideas.

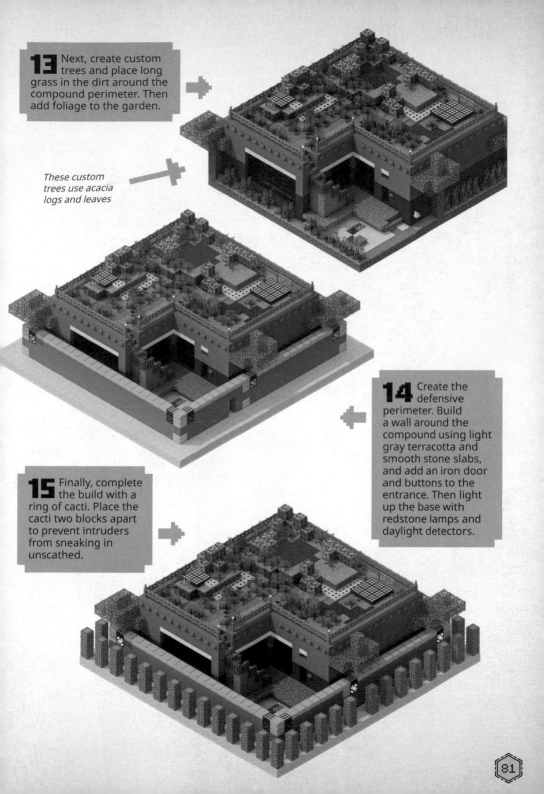

13 Next, create custom trees and place long grass in the dirt around the compound perimeter. Then add foliage to the garden.

These custom trees use acacia logs and leaves

14 Create the defensive perimeter. Build a wall around the compound using light gray terracotta and smooth stone slabs, and add an iron door and buttons to the entrance. Then light up the base with redstone lamps and daylight detectors.

15 Finally, complete the build with a ring of cacti. Place the cacti two blocks apart to prevent intruders from sneaking in unscathed.

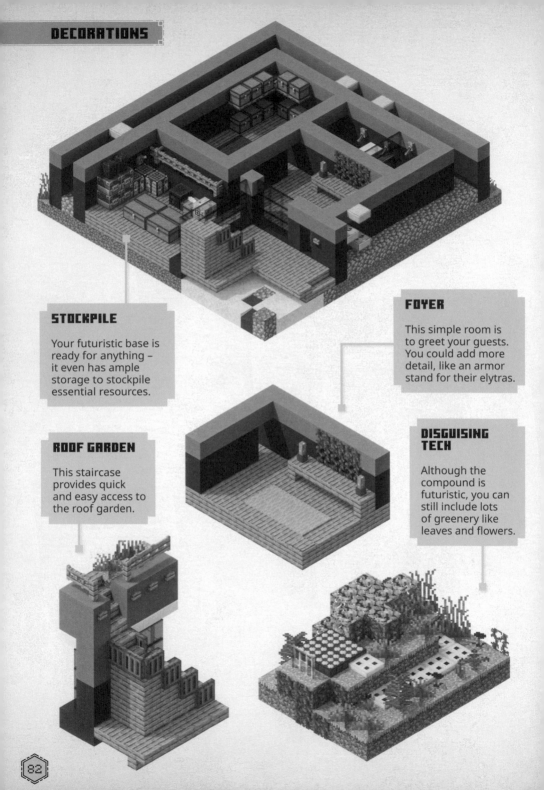

STOCKPILE

Your futuristic base is ready for anything – it even has ample storage to stockpile essential resources.

FOYER

This simple room is to greet your guests. You could add more detail, like an armor stand for their elytras.

ROOF GARDEN

This staircase provides quick and easy access to the roof garden.

DISGUISING TECH

Although the compound is futuristic, you can still include lots of greenery like leaves and flowers.

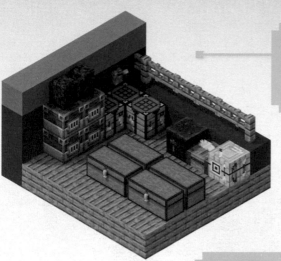

JOB BLOCKS

Keep your most-used job blocks within easy reach so you can prepare all your building materials in one go.

ENTRANCE

Protect the entrance with cacti and an iron door. Cactus can only be placed on sand or red sand.

WET ROOM

Bathrooms can be super simple. This design is for a wet room, complete with a waterhole and sink.

LIVING SPACE

This compound is designed for survival, not comfort! Be sure to have your supplies close to hand with nearby chests, so you can be ready at a moment's notice.

"Like many of our generation, we're inspired to make the world a better place. A major issue we face is global warming, so we thought: How could we change this? Together, we decided to make the main source of carbon dioxide our inspiration: factories.

"Steam engines were invented in the early 1800s, and by the 1850s, factories were using them as a means for efficient production." This industrial factory uses the gray hues of stone and cobblestone to create the chambers.

"Nowadays, we know that the pollution caused by factories can be deadly, so we designed an advanced filtration system." This system contains the gases within red sandstone and granite pipes, and redirects excess heat to nearby homes.

Finding inspiration for new builds can be tough, so we've asked the professional build team Varuna to share how they take a simple idea and develop it into a large-scale build. We decided to challenge them to create a build that would make the world a better place. Here is their creation.

Industrial plants like these produce lots and lots of excess heat. Once purified, the hot gases are redirected via underground pipes to heat nearby homes. The pipes are reinforced with cobblestone walls to ensure no dangerous gases leak into the environment.

This filtration system is built using andesite and blocks of iron. Each chamber further filters the gases, so that our planet stays healthy.

"Steam engines run on compressed steam. If you look closely, you can see the tubes where hot air passes through to the metallic chambers." The tubes are made using Nether bricks to create a dirty, soot-covered look.

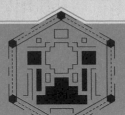

MEDIEVAL MANOR

MAIN BLOCKS

FRONT

SIDE

TOP

Now that you've completed a few builds, it's time for you to take the next step. You can develop your builds to be as large as you like, just ensure they follow your theme. Let's look at how to create a medieval manor. When you're finished, see if you can turn your build into an entire hamlet!

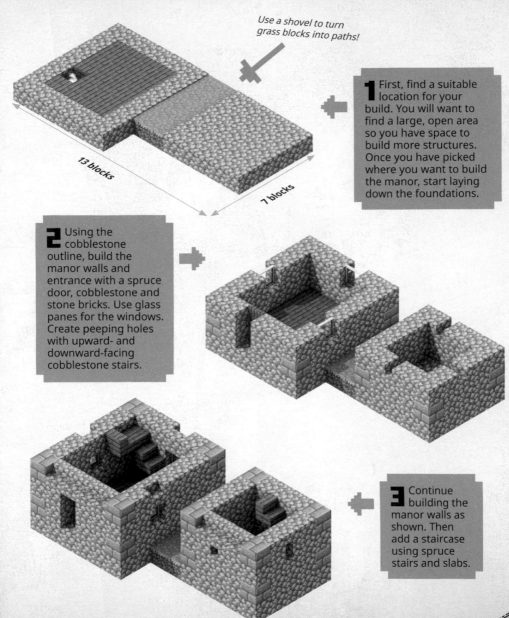

Use a shovel to turn grass blocks into paths!

13 blocks

7 blocks

1 First, find a suitable location for your build. You will want to find a large, open area so you have space to build more structures. Once you have picked where you want to build the manor, start laying down the foundations.

2 Using the cobblestone outline, build the manor walls and entrance with a spruce door, cobblestone and stone bricks. Use glass panes for the windows. Create peeping holes with upward- and downward-facing cobblestone stairs.

3 Continue building the manor walls as shown. Then add a staircase using spruce stairs and slabs.

4 Next, join the two buildings together with another floor. Add the new floor above the stairs using spruce slabs, logs and cobblestone. Use buttons and fences to decorate.

5 Extend the walls by two blocks as shown, using a mix of spruce logs and diorite for a half-timbered architectural style. Add plenty of windows to fill the room with daylight.

6 Next, start building the shape of the roofs. Use spruce logs and diorite to create the triangular shape for two roofs as shown.

See page 39 for more information on triangular prisms.

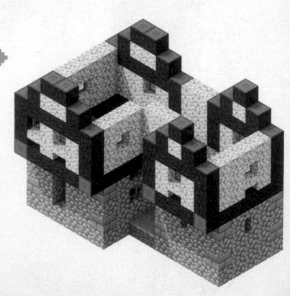

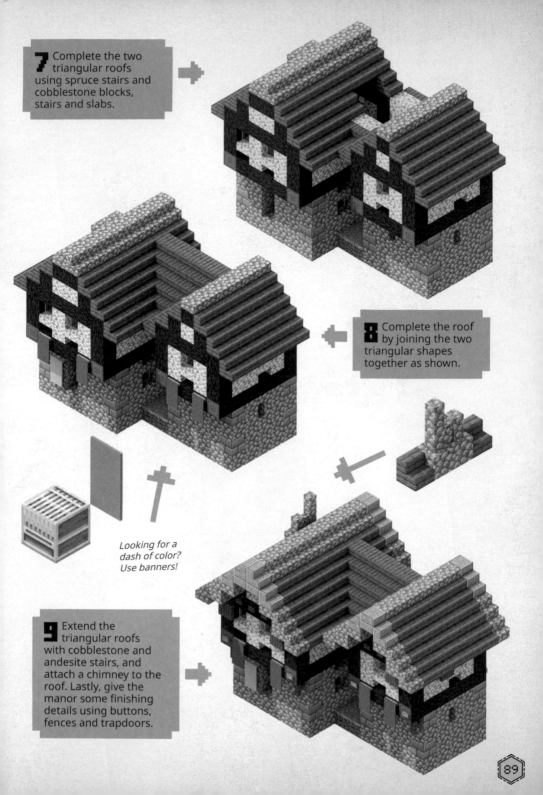

7 Complete the two triangular roofs using spruce stairs and cobblestone blocks, stairs and slabs.

8 Complete the roof by joining the two triangular shapes together as shown.

Looking for a dash of color? Use banners!

9 Extend the triangular roofs with cobblestone and andesite stairs, and attach a chimney to the roof. Lastly, give the manor some finishing details using buttons, fences and trapdoors.

89

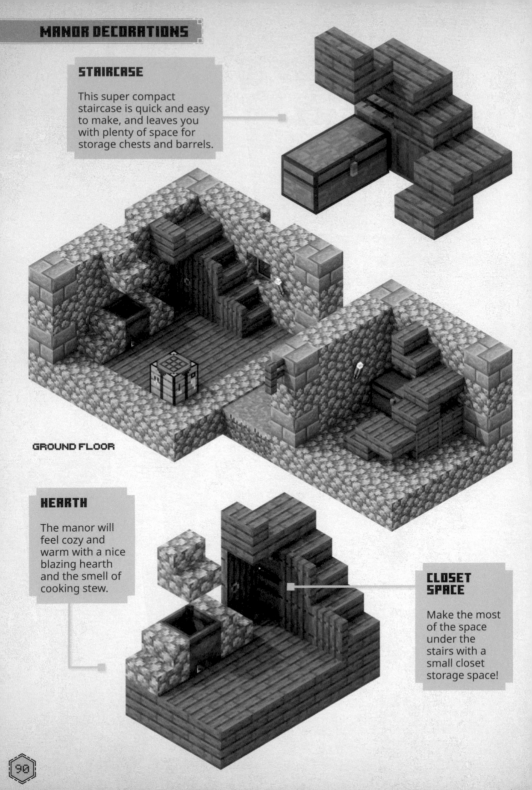

STAIRCASE

This super compact staircase is quick and easy to make, and leaves you with plenty of space for storage chests and barrels.

GROUND FLOOR

HEARTH

The manor will feel cozy and warm with a nice blazing hearth and the smell of cooking stew.

CLOSET SPACE

Make the most of the space under the stairs with a small closet storage space!

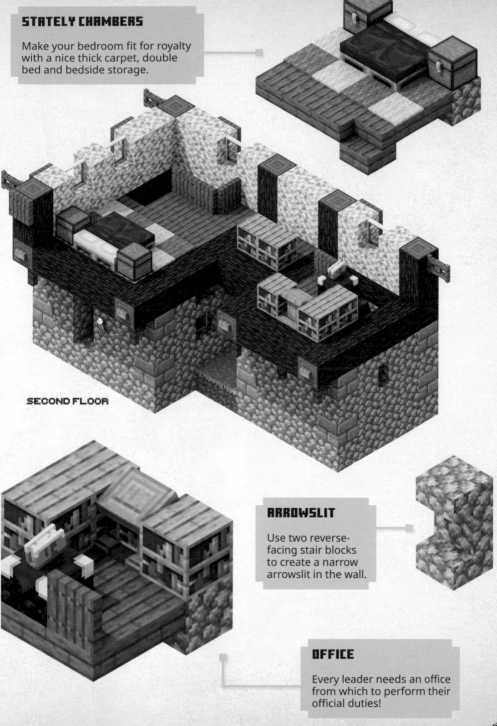

STATELY CHAMBERS

Make your bedroom fit for royalty with a nice thick carpet, double bed and bedside storage.

SECOND FLOOR

ARROWSLIT

Use two reverse-facing stair blocks to create a narrow arrowslit in the wall.

OFFICE

Every leader needs an office from which to perform their official duties!

Once you've completed the manor, try developing your build into a complete medieval hamlet. There are lots of things you can include, from watchtowers and market stalls to wagons and bridges. What will you create?

MARKET STALL

Market stalls are evidence of a thriving community. Villagers will trade resources for useful items.

WATCHTOWER

With pillagers wandering about, searching for villages to raid, it's prudent to keep an eye out for danger. A watchtower will give you a high vantage point to spot danger from a mile away!

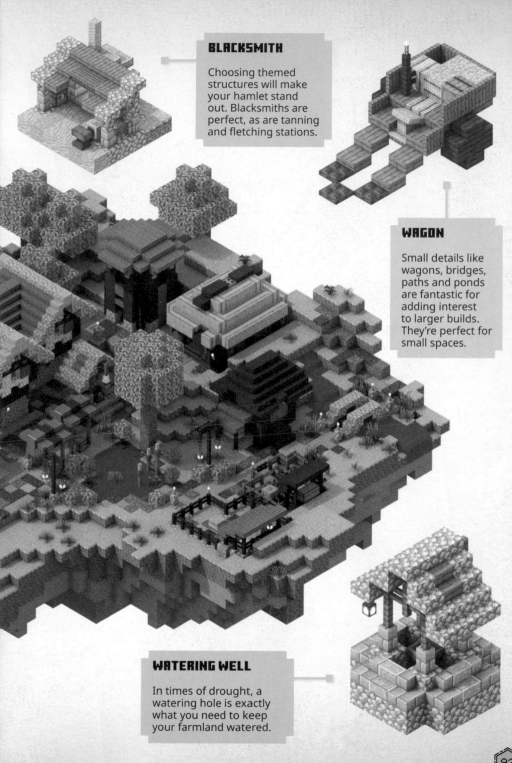

BLACKSMITH

Choosing themed structures will make your hamlet stand out. Blacksmiths are perfect, as are tanning and fletching stations.

WAGON

Small details like wagons, bridges, paths and ponds are fantastic for adding interest to larger builds. They're perfect for small spaces.

WATERING WELL

In times of drought, a watering hole is exactly what you need to keep your farmland watered.

GOODBYE

Well, that's it! You've made it to the end of *Minecraft: Guide to Creative!* We hope you've learned a thing or two, and that your brain is fizzing with ideas and new things to try. But before you go, we've got one last lesson. Actually, maybe it's the most important one.

Don't stop with what you've read here!

There's no right or wrong way to build, and you're doing the right thing so long as you're having fun. The expert knowledge and build guides between these pages are a great way to get started, and now that you're finished, it's up to you to put your new skills to the test in creating amazing builds.

But you're not alone. There are countless resources available on the Minecraft website, Marketplace and wiki, and it's perfectly okay to look around to find inspiration. Don't get disheartened if your builds don't yet quite compare – the best ones take months to complete, even with entire teams of builders. And they all had to start somewhere.

OK, NOW WE'RE REALLY DONE. WHAT ARE YOU WAITING FOR? GET CREATIVE! WE CAN'T WAIT TO SEE WHAT YOU BUILD!

DISCOVER MORE MINECRAFT:
LEVEL UP YOUR GAME WITH THE OFFICIAL GUIDES

- ☐ *GUIDE TO COMBAT*
- ☐ *GUIDE TO CREATIVE*
- ☐ *GUIDE TO ENCHANTMENTS & POTIONS*
- ☐ *GUIDE TO FARMING*
- ☐ *GUIDE TO MINECRAFT DUNGEONS*

- ☐ *GUIDE TO OCEAN SURVIVAL*
- ☐ *GUIDE TO THE NETHER & THE END*
- ☐ *GUIDE TO PVP MINIGAMES*
- ☐ *GUIDE TO REDSTONE*
- ☐ *GUIDE TO SURVIVAL*

MORE MINECRAFT:

- ☐ *EPIC BASES*
- ☐ *EXPLODED BUILDS: MEDIEVAL FORTRESS*
- ☐ *LET'S BUILD! LAND OF ZOMBIES*
- ☐ *LET'S BUILD! THEME PARK ADVENTURE*

- ☐ *MAPS*
- ☐ *MINECRAFT FOR BEGINNERS*
- ☐ *MOBESTIARY*
- ☐ *THE SURVIVORS' BOOK OF SECRETS*

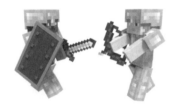

Penguin
Random
House